Shark Tank Secrets!

By Rob Gramer

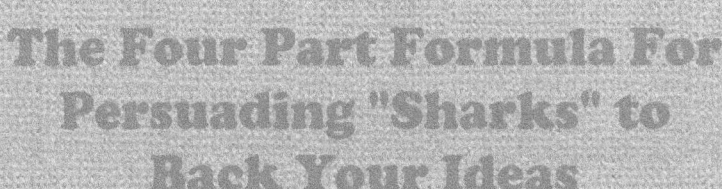

The Four Part Formula For Persuading "Sharks" to Back Your Ideas

Go to www.inventionprep.com to learn how to start profiting off your idea in the next 30 days.

Inside:

Go to www.inventionprep.com to learn how to start profiting off your idea in the next 30 days.

Go to www.inventionprep.com to learn how to start profiting off your idea in the next 30 days.

Go to www.inventionprep.com to learn how to start profiting off your idea in the next 30 days.

Introduction

The Legendary Thomas Edison's Definition of a Successful Invention

If your goal is to have all of the money you need to bring your inventions to life and to have them sell like hotcakes out in the marketplace, don't read this book...*memorize* it.

This book reveals in detail a very powerful strategy for persuading investors to fund your new products, inventions, and ideas. It will change the way you think about approaching investors. It will change the way you present your ideas to them. It will save you time. It will give you more resources for making every single one of your inventions a reality.

Learn this strategy and you will never worry about having enough money. How much cash you have to fund your dreams is entirely up to you. Because if you use the techniques I lay out in this report haphazardly you may get a few bucks here and there. When executed properly, you'll have investors fighting each other for the right to back your idea.

I can say this with confidence for three reasons:

First, there is a method to the madness to getting a product backed and to market. And because of my

Go to www.inventionprep.com to learn how to start profiting off your idea in the next 30 days.

work in a law office that specializes in patents, I speak with tinkerers, inventors, and innovative business owners every day. I see what works...what doesn't work...and what separates the people who see their dreams comes true from the ones who constantly face frustration and failure.

Second, there is a pattern to who gets funding and who walks away empty handed. Supplementing my findings working with inventors, I've watched and studied every episode of the hit ABC show **Shark Tank** (the reality TV show where inventors present their ideas to investors - called **Sharks** - and try to convince them to invest money in their ideas). Amazingly, the exact elements that consistently help the inventors who walk through my office, work like gangbusters for the inventors who secure a deal from the **Sharks**.

And finally, I've spent much of my career making and selling the things I've developed, (we'll talk more about that in a second).

If you learn the strategy I outline in this report - and it can easily be learned - you can expect certain immediate benefits.

- It will be easier to find investors
- They will be more receptive to what you have to say

Go to www.inventionprep.com to learn how to start profiting off your idea in the next 30 days.

7

- Turning you down will seem like they are actually throwing away money, rather than taking a bet on you
- You will give up less equity in your company
- They will invest more, and more often
- Your ideas will be designed, prototyped, and on the market quicker than you ever dreamed possible

I can promise you all of this with confidence because most inventors make a huge mistake that dooms them to wasting tons of time and money on inventions that no one will ever buy. And if no one will ever buy your inventions, how can you expect to grow rich off of them?

What Dooms Inventors to Failure

In the following pages, I will expose what this big mistake is...why inventors make it...how it kills your chances of finding financial backing for your idea...and actually kills the creative spirit inside of you. This is the #1 reason why smart, hard working, and gifted inventors are considered "failures" by their family and friends (if you've ever wanted to give up on your ideas, I guarantee you are making this mistake).

Not only will this change how you look at inventing forever, it will also help you create new products in record time. Instead of spending years developing

Go to www.inventionprep.com to learn how to start profiting off your idea in the next 30 days.

8

something new, you'll be able to get it done in months, sometimes weeks. And these will be products that you KNOW will sell before you spend one minute...or one penny...developing them.

You should be able to read this book in less than an hour. It is important you read this entire book beginning to end because in it you will discover how to save TONS of time, energy, and money (This is the key to being an inventor who has lots of products selling in the marketplace and NOT the inventor who jumps around from product to product, never getting anything out there).

By this time tomorrow, you will have a persuasive tool not one in one thousand inventors have. But, I recommend you reread this book several times during the next few weeks. With each reading, new secrets will be opened up for you.

By keeping this book as a personal resource, you won't have to worry about forgetting any of the details (I've also included a handy checklist in the appendix). Everything you need to understand this strategy and put it into action is contained in the following pages.

How I Discovered this Breakthrough Strategy

Like I mentioned above, my background is in mechanical engineering. Specifically, I used to design

Go to www.inventionprep.com to learn how to start profiting off your idea in the next 30 days.

9

jet engines. I've worked with big firms like Boeing, Lockheed Martin, Pratt and Whitney, Sikorsky, and the ultra secretive Defense Advanced Research Projects Agency.

I was a damn good engineer, but I hated dealing with government contract work (too much bureaucracy!). So when my employer asked me to start a business with him I jumped at the opportunity. But a good engineer does not make a good businessman. Shortly after he hired me, I was instrumental in driving the business into the ground and wasting about half a million dollars in the process.

Up until that point, I'd spent my entire life learning the craft of designing and creating things. I could tear down and fix a motorcycle, build an addition on a house, or design an engine powerful enough for a 747. But I didn't know why people buy. I'd never given one moment of thought to why people hand over their cold, hard cash for anything. And because of this I could make almost anything, but found it hard to find customers for my creations.

From that day forward, I vowed to learn how to "sell" things.

A lot of people (especially inventors), think "selling" is a dirty word. "I shouldn't have to sell my product," they say, "it is so good it sells itself!"

Go to www.inventionprep.com to learn how to start profiting off your idea in the next 30 days.

I agree that "selling" in the form of pushing people to buy something they do not want is a bad thing. However, that is not the type of "selling" I am talking about here. Once I learned how to do this (and the strategy I'm about to reveal to you), it was off to the races. Since then I've been involved in multiple successful businesses including, home electronics, construction, offshore bank account and second citizenship advice, tax accounting software, martial arts DVD's, weight loss plans, cookware, and on and on. I've watched things I've created succeed in the marketplace. I've made a lot more money.

Why Most Inventors Fail

This is very, very important. And I believe that this is the one thing that differentiates the rich, successful inventor from the inventors with thousands of "ideas" but nothing being sold.

It has to do with your brain. And how it is "wired" differently than most people. Don't worry! This isn't necessarily a bad thing. On one hand it can help you be more creative. But if you aren't careful it can kill your chances to persuade investors to back your idea (or drive you to work on projects that won't make you any money).

Here's how it kept me poor for years...

Go to www.inventionprep.com to learn how to start profiting off your idea in the next 30 days.

11

You see, I grew up playing with Legos and chemistry sets. Hammers, wrenches, and screwdrivers were my birthday gifts. More than once I salvaged broken lawnmowers from the neighbor's trash so I could rip them apart and figure out how they worked. When I wanted a skateboard ramp, I built a 4 foot tall half pipe. And most of my allowance went to paying for late fees on library books about physics, space flight, and other scientific stuff normal kids just don't think or read about.

I had a thirst for knowledge on HOW things work.

This will come as a shock to most inventors, but most people could care less about the inner workings of most things. They don't want to know why an air conditioner blows cold air or how a remote control changes channels. The only thing they care about is cold air and keeping their butts planted on the couch instead of walking to the TV every time a commercial comes on.

The reality is most people do not care how things work, they just want to know what it will do for them. How will it make their lives easier? How will it simplify their daily routines? How will it help them do things faster? How can it save them money?

Once I finally realized (and this was very painful for me) that people don't care about how things work,

Go to www.inventionprep.com to learn how to start profiting off your idea in the next 30 days.

12

but instead what those things will do for them, my income exploded.

How to Invent Things People Want to Buy

Selling your ideas was not talked about much when I was in engineering school. Back then, the teachers talked about formulas...Newton's Laws of Motion...how to calculate how strong a beam must be to hold up a building...how much air flow you need to run an engine...etc.

These formulas are what engineers use to build bridges, automobiles, towering skyscrapers, and the space shuttle that put a man on the moon.

But did you know there are formulas for selling things to? And that if you simply follow these formulas selling your ideas and inventions becomes a breeze. In the sections that follow, I will walk you through this simple four part formula. To put it to work for you, I will teach you a few important strategies.

- **Why rich inventors always focus on "Entrepreneurial Alchemy" instead of how their product works when pitching their ideas**
- The three factors investors evaluate before they decide to fund your project

Go to www.inventionprep.com to learn how to start profiting off your idea in the next 30 days.

13

- **How one of my early employers made $91,000 a year with employees who would start work by drinking a few beers...break numerous laws all throughout the night ...and would spend the last hour on the job chasing drunk girls. Required reading for smart people who can't seem to get rich**
- How stealing smart supercharges your ability to persuade investors to back your idea
- **The deal breaker that forces investors to walk away even if they love your product (and the dealmaker that attracts investors like bees to honey even if you have a subpar product)**
- What snipers can teach you about putting together a bullet proof pitch
- **When being a slick salesman kills your chances for funding and how to create a product that sells itself**
- The first step you must take before putting together your pitch (in fact, if you do this first you will never again waste time and money inventing a dud)
- **How to avoid inventing something that people don't want to buy**
- The inconvenient truths about money: Why good, smart people stay poor and evil, dumb people grow rich.
- **And finally, the four elements to a bulletproof pitch! Used by every winner and**

Go to www.inventionprep.com to learn how to start profiting off your idea in the next 30 days.

14

ignored by every loser on Shark Tank, the step-by-step formula is the key to persuading investors to back your idea.

This is how the report is arranged. There are three sections which explain these concepts in detail with plenty of examples.

The strategy you are about to learn will easily help you find funding for your idea. More likely, if you are an active inventor, what you're about to learn could easily be the difference between another idea stuck in your head (or prototype gathering dust in your garage) and a product on store shelves across the world helping millions of people.

How this can happen is quite simple. This strategy makes you invent things people can't help to see the value in their heads...want to buy...want to invest in...want to be a part of - *before* you spend countless hours and thousands of dollars on the end product. Which means you won't be "selling" investors on your idea. They will automatically see the value in your invention. Many times they will think it is MORE valuable than you say it is.

Put it all together and this means less frustration and work for you, with your products getting on shelves quicker, and royalties flowing in.

Here's how the legendary inventor Thomas Edison put it:

Go to www.inventionprep.com to learn how to start profiting off your idea in the next 30 days.

15

"Anything that won't sell, I don't want to invent. Its sale is proof of utility, and utility is success" - Thomas Edison

The report you're holding represents a tiny investment compared to what you stand to earn using this strategy. All you have to do now - to turn the ideas in your head into a financial windfall - is to read on and pay attention to what you are reading...and then to put it into action.

But that's easy, as you'll see as you continue reading...

Go to www.inventionprep.com to learn how to start profiting off your idea in the next 30 days.

16

Part 1: What is Your Idea, Your Dream, Your Baby...Worth?

When Having NO Sales is Better than a Booming Business. Entrepreneurial Alchemy and the Three P's of Inventor Financing

If you haven't sold one single item, then I have good news for you. You may be in a better position to convince investors to back your idea than someone who has pushed hundreds or thousands of dollars worth of product.

Allow me to explain...

There are two ways to place a dollar figure on a company or product.

First, the sales and profit margin over time, what most people call a "track record". For example, let's say you've sold $50,000 worth of widgets over the last year. And from those sales, you've netted a $25,000 profit. If so, then it is within the realm of possibility that if you do the same thing next year, you will net another $25,000. The valuation of the company is easy. $25,000 per year.

Go to www.inventionprep.com to learn how to start profiting off your idea in the next 30 days.

17

But you can't do this math is you haven't made a single sale. Zero multiplied by zero is always nothing. Yet every day new products are introduced that go from a few sales the first year...to a million the next year...to $10 million and beyond after that.

So, what if that is you? What if you are at square one? And you haven't sold a single widget? What if you have sunk thousands of dollars into developing your product? And not a single customer, sale, or purchase order? What if your idea is completely new? But you know you have a rockstar product in the making in your hands?

If that is you, then I have good news. Not having sales can be much, much better for you. By taking the focus off of facts like sales, cost of doing business, or profit margins, you can make your value argument based on something OTHER than facts and "hard math".

I call this Entrepreneurial Alchemy. Done properly this is a huge asset for inventors. Many times you can get more cash from investors...while also giving up less of the equity of your company. There are secrets to Entrepreneurial Alchemy in this section (and sprinkled throughout this report).

We will talk more about this in a second. But before we dive in, let's get a little perspective of the

Go to www.inventionprep.com to learn how to start profiting off your idea in the next 30 days.

18

investor mindset by taking a closer look at how the *Sharks* evaluate products that do have sales.

So You've Got Sales...The Questions

After watching nearly every episode of *Shark Tank* I've identified 27 questions that each of the *Sharks* ask on a consistent basis. Nine of these questions have directly to do with 'hard' data likes sales and profit margins.

Those nine questions are:

1. How much in sales do you have?
2. How long did it take to make those sales?
3. What were the sales first year, next year, year after that, etc.?
4. What's the margin?
5. How much do you have in unfilled orders?
6. Where are you selling this?
7. What's your profit margin (cost to make vs. cost to sell – sell to retail or end user)?
8. What's your projection for sales (1 year from now…2 years from now, etc.)?
9. And the best question – Would you sell the whole business?

If you can answer these questions with solid numbers, your job of swaying the *Sharks* to invest

Go to www.inventionprep.com to learn how to start profiting off your idea in the next 30 days.

with you should not be that difficult. You must simply give them enough of a controlling stake or royalty to make the return on investment worthwhile.

That's fine if you've got a proven product, but how do you sway the **Sharks** if sales are low or not there at all?

This happened to Kevin and Melissa Kiernan with their Last Lid product, a universal trash can replacement lid (they had lost their original trash cans lids and couldn't find replacements). Raccoons would invade their trash at night, eat garbage and generally make a mess.

So they devised their own lid out of raccoon proof fabric that secured to the top of the trash can. The **Shark Tank** burst out into laughter. Who would buy a replacement lid? Why not just buy another trash can? They all declined to invest, except for Daymond.

What changed Daymond's mind? It was simply the fact that a few months prior he lost the lid to his trash can. He recounted the story of searching online and in stores for a replacement lid with no luck.

The result?

Daymond ended up investing $40,000 for 60% of the company EVEN THOUGHT THEY HADN'T SOLD ONE SINGLE CAN TOP! For piece of fabric with nothing more than a draw string, imagine pocketing

Go to www.inventionprep.com to learn how to start profiting off your idea in the next 30 days.

sixty grand for a simple invention like that! (Granted, they gave away a controlling stake in the company...but with zero sales, they didn't own anything. 40% of something is better than 100% of nothing.)

Entrepreneurial Alchemy

The story of Last Lid securing funding illustrates the key to swaying investors without "showing them the money".

I call this secret Entrepreneurial Alchemy. Alchemy is the ancient belief you can turn cheap, base metals into precious gold. It is chemically impossible. But Kevin and Melissa Kiernan performed Entrepreneurial Alchemy with their Last Lid product. They took something fairly worthless - a piece of fabric with a draw string - and turned it into $40,000. How?

You perform Entrepreneurial Alchemy when you help people see the bright future laid out before them if they buy into your idea...bankroll your invention...or purchase your product.

Daymond saw a need for the trash can top that the other **Sharks** did not. If he – a multimillionaire – couldn't find a replacement trash can top, I'm sure he imagined (this is an important word, imagined) hundreds and thousands of other people, perhaps

Go to www.inventionprep.com to learn how to start profiting off your idea in the next 30 days.

millions, searching as well. This imagination...this VISION is what drove him to invest. Even when his fellow **Sharks** were mocking him.

Creating VISION of how you idea/invention/product will be like an atomic bomb going off in the marketplace....creating VISION of endless crowds of people clamoring for your product...creating VISION of orders, sales, boatloads of cash flooding in is the key to swaying investors to back you if you have no sales. This ability to create VISION is the driving power behind Entrepreneurial Alchemy.

It is essential then that you create VISION. If the reality is that you have no sales, you must create the picture for the **Sharks**. You must show them how many people are in the marketplace. How much they are willing to spend. How valuable your product is. And how many people will pay good money for it. And why you will hustle like a crack-head fiending for a fix to make it a reality.

This is how Joe Moore coaxed a $4 MILLION dollar complete buy-out offer (the most in the history of **Shark Tank**) out of Robert Herjavec.

What is more impressive is this monstrous sum was for a product no more complex than a band-aid. First Defense Nasal Screen is a small adhesive air filter you stick over your nostrils. It prevents dust and

Go to www.inventionprep.com to learn how to start profiting off your idea in the next 30 days.

22

contaminates from entering the nasal passage. Moore had zero sales (although he did have a large purchase order) and had sunk hundreds of thousand into product development and patent protection.

When I saw First Defense Nasal Screens I thought it was a silly idea...and so did all of the **Sharks**. But then Moore explained how horrible air quality is around the world. And how millions (if not billions) of people use those strap on air filters that cover half your face. Now here was a product that worked better than those air filters...was not as noticeable (because it covered just the nostrils, not the entire nose, mouth, and chin)...and could probably be produced for less money.

Slowly, he created the VISION of millions of people switching from air filters to his Nasal Screens. The **Sharks** stopped laughing and went into a bidding war for his product.

This is the power of creating vision.

In the rest of this report, you will learn the art of Entrepreneurial Alchemy and how to create vision. And the first thing you must know is that the vision doesn't always have to come from your product.

I have no doubt First Defense Nasal Screens will sell billions of units (and help a good deal of people around the world to breathe easier). But you don't necessarily need a great product to secure financing. Go to www.inventionprep.com to learn how to start profiting off your idea in the next 30 days.

I've identified three factors - which I call **The Three P's of Inventor Financing** - which help you convince investors you know what you are talking about. We've already talked about the first one, having a great product. Let's take a closer look at the second two.

The Three P's of Inventor Financing

Does having a great product and proven sales always ensure you'll sway the **Sharks**?

Not if you make the same mistake Donny McCall made.

His Invis-A-Rack system- a organizational rack for a truck that folds away, unseen, when not in use - got rave reviews. To boot, he had proven sales in a segment of the market that was growing (pickup trucks). In fact, he had such a powerful pitch it brought Robert Herjavec to tears!

But in the end, none of the **Sharks** invested. Why?

Because Donny McCall swore up and down he would never let his product be manufactured out of the U.S. And the only way the **Sharks** thought it would be profitable to make this product would be overseas production. So besides a great product, a genuine person behind it, and an impassioned pitch, all the **Sharks** declined to invest.

Go to www.inventionprep.com to learn how to start profiting off your idea in the next 30 days.

This illustrates an important point, if The **Sharks** do not like YOUR PLAN, they will not invest. You see this time and again on the **Shark Tank**. An inventor will have a great product, but no way to make it financially feasible, and everyone will bow out. The second P in **The Three P's of Inventor Financing** stands for Plan.

When the **Sharks** are interested in your plan, you'll hear questions like:

- What are you going to do in 5 years?
- When does your target need this product?
- How will you get there?
- Walk me through how it works?
- What would you do with the money?
- Where do you want to sell this?
- Do you make this yourself or with help?

Notice here they are asking questions about the future of your manufacturing procedure...when the customer will need your product...your ideas about how the investment money should be used...and how you plan to sell and market your invention.

They want to know about your plans for manufacturing...how much research you've done into your target customer...and your sales and marketing plan.

Go to www.inventionprep.com to learn how to start profiting off your idea in the next 30 days.

Sounds like a lot of hard work, right?

Ethical "Stealing" For Easy and Quick Profit

Well, I've got a way to make coming up with these plans super easy for you. It will save you countless hours of time. Give you the most foolproof, proven successful plans possible. Plus, it will give the **Sharks** a greater incentive to invest with you.

All you have to do is simply adopt one the already successful plans of one of the **Sharks**.

This works like gangbusters because, then, you are not trying to pitch a brand new, unproven (possibly risky) product or idea...but a new twist on something that is, to them, successful, and already proven.

Remember what I said about VISION above? About how you must create the picture for the **Sharks**, so they can see the bright future that lay ahead of them? Well, you can accomplish this by borrowing on the success of one of their plans...either the way they manufacture...how they distribute product...or their sales and marketing approach...and show how your idea complements what they are already doing.

Go to www.inventionprep.com to learn how to start profiting off your idea in the next 30 days.

Consider the story of Rick Hopper. He had a simple idea: ReadeRest, a small, magnetic clip attached to the shirt to keep reading glasses in place when not in use. He came up with the idea when he kept on losing reading glasses.

When he presented the idea on **Shark Tank**, most of the **Sharks** rolled their eyes. ReadeRest is nothing more than a couple of magnets and a piece of wire. Who would buy a cheap little product like that?

Where the other **Sharks** saw nothing. Lori Greiner saw opportunity.

Dubbed the Queen of TV shopping channel QVC, Lori had sold hundreds of thousands of pairs of reading glasses. She immediately saw an opportunity to "bundle" the eyeglass holder with the reading glasses she already sold. She tossed an offer of $150,000 for 65% of the company and Hopper took it.

In an interview with Hopper, he mentioned how he researched the **Sharks**, and decided to focus on trying to sell Greiner on his invention BEFORE going on the show.

I share with you this story because there was nothing particularly revolutionary about Hoppers product, but it fit into how Lori sells her products - direct through TV (this is one reason why it is so important to know the background of the people you are pitching your ideas to, more on that in a moment). Go to www.inventionprep.com to learn how to start profiting off your idea in the next 30 days.

27

The Deal Breaker

Nothing will stop an investor from funding you faster than this third P in *The Three P's of Investor Financing*. It will kill you dead in your tracks even if you have a stellar product and a rock-solid plan. Get this wrong, and the *Sharks* will pass.

Do you remember Donny McCall and the Invis-A-Rack system from earlier in this report? Recall how the *Sharks* passed on his product - the organizational rack for a truck that folds away, unseen, when not in use - after he swore up and down he would never let his product be manufactured out of the U.S. Immediately after that comment, Barbara Corcoran bowed out. She told him a good entrepreneur has to be open-minded to all options when growing a business. And that his stubbornness about manufacturing offshore would eventually kill the business.

She didn't like him.

The final P in *The Three P's of Inventor Financing* is personal...YOU! How much faith does the investor have in you to get things done? Do you have a personal track record of accomplishment? Do you have the right attitude? The right credentials? Do they like (or hate) you?

Go to www.inventionprep.com to learn how to start profiting off your idea in the next 30 days.

And can you blame them? Nobody wants to work with someone who is incompetent, doesn't pull their weight, or is simply a pain in the ass to be around. You can tell if the **Sharks** are evaluating YOU if they ask you any of the following questions:

- What is your motivation?
- How did you get into this business?
- How much of your own time/money have you put into it?
- Have you gone to a bank to try and get money?
- Have you paid yourself?

When the **Sharks** ask questions like these, they are trying to figure out what skills you bring to the table. And the wrong answers usually lead to you walking away empty handed.

This is what happened to Amanda Schlechter. Her idea (which I thought was quite clever) was the Ledge Pillow, a triangular shaped pillow that made it comfortable for large breasted women to sleep on their stomachs in comfort. But the **Sharks** discovered she only sold 83 units in 3 years. After all the **Sharks** bowed out, Mark Cuban said she didn't have any sales because she didn't want it bad enough. And then said, "I'm out".

YOU are a big part of the equation. Bad personality traits are usually a deal breaker. Show

Go to www.inventionprep.com to learn how to start profiting off your idea in the next 30 days.

29

yourself to be lazy, stubborn, arrogant, aloof, indecisive, narrow minded, unreliable, weak-willed, or just plain stupid and you can kiss a deal from the *Sharks* goodbye.

The Deal Maker

But it works both ways. If you display the right personality, sometimes you can have a so-so product, or a questionable plan and still find backing.

This is fantastic news. You can have a crummy product, but if you've pushed it to the limit (through sales, securing retail distribution, or strategic partnerships) from your own blood, sweat, and tears the *Sharks* will happily give you the money simply because they believe in YOU and want you to be a part of their businesses. Your personality can even save you if everything else sucks.

Four brothers founded a company around a sunburn relief cream called Nardo's Naturals. There was nothing extraordinary about the product. They had no sales. And Barbara Corcoran scoffed at them, "Your projection for $4.8 million in sales with no justification of how to get there really makes us have to be foolish to believe you." Do you know what she did next? She gave them $75,000 for 50%! Why? Because during the pitch, they all talked about mom and how she was the inspiration for their idea! And Barbara loved the fact these four "manly" brothers

Go to www.inventionprep.com to learn how to start profiting off your idea in the next 30 days.

started a company around such a "feminine" product. Plus, she explained, what's better than getting four hard working guys for the price of one?

Steve Gadlin's "I Want to Draw a Cat for You" service (you tell him what you want, and he will create a stick figure cat drawing of it for $9.95) was probably the most ridiculous thing I've ever seen. Yet Mark Cuban cut him a check for $25,000 in exchange for a 33% stake in the company. On the episode, Mark explained you can't just find a guy with creative energy like that. Mark didn't buy the product, he bought the guy. (It's also worthy to note that Steve mentioned on his blog that Mark, "Pitch(s) in with ideas and advice far more than you'd expect.")

Hill Billy - a clothing line targeted at the country music set - was nothing out of the ordinary. But the founders Mike Abbaticchio and Shon Less caught the eye of Jeff Foxworhty. Selling the t-shirts out of the back of their van at concerts, and owning the trademark "Hill Billy" was enough to coax $75,000 for a 7% royalty out of Jeff Foxworthy, Daymond John, and Robert Herjavec.

The key takeaway from these examples is that you must be stellar. So make sure that your passion, drive, and ability to get things done comes through in your pitch.

Go to www.inventionprep.com to learn how to start profiting off your idea in the next 30 days.

31

To recap, the Three P's of Inventor Financing stand for Product, Plan, and Personal (You). Demonstrate competence in all three, and you are well on your way to success. However, you can have all three of these in place, but it won't amount to a hill of beans if your pitch is delivered to deaf ears.

Go to www.inventionprep.com to learn how to start profiting off your idea in the next 30 days.

32

Part 2: How Can You Go Forward If You Don't Know Which Way You Are Facing?

What Snipers Can Teach You About Securing Funded if You Hate Sales and The Aqueduct Factors for Money Flow

This next section illustrates one of the biggest reasons why otherwise good ideas, plans, and people fail to find funding. It dawned upon me while firing some rounds off at the shooting range the other day.

Fun factoid: Did you know the record for longest kill shot in battle stands at 2,430 meters? For those in the U.S., that is roughly a mile and a half...or 26 football fields in length!

At that distance gravity causes the bullet to fall. Wind blows it off course. Humidity and barometric pressure can slow it down. Even the rotation of the earth - the Coriolis Effect - comes into play (at 900 meters, it will push the bullet a full three inches off target...or a little less than 9 inches for our world record shooting sniper). Hitting your mark, then, is NOT just about looking through a scope and pulling the trigger.

Go to www.inventionprep.com to learn how to start profiting off your idea in the next 30 days.

33

What does this have to do with you?

When pitching your product you must know WHO you are targeting. Not everyone will respond to your pitch (obviously, you could deliver a grand slam pitch to a homeless man, but he would not have the funding to make your idea a reality). The who - the target - is extremely important.

And part of "the who" that is frequently overlooked is HOW they will respond to your pitch. Just like gravity, wind, pressure, rotation of the earth, etc. will knock a bullet off target, there are factors that will influence how someone responds to your pitch. You see this all the time on the **Shark Tank**. An inventor pitches a great product, and the **Sharks** bow out because it doesn't fit into their business model or knowledge base.

But when you communicate the value of your product in such a way that resonates with the person you are pitching it to, magical things happen. Instead of doubting you, your plan, or your idea they will start to find ways to get it to fit into their business model. This may be small at first...a slight, "hmmm" while they think how it could work. Then something more promising like a suggestion, "Have you thought about selling it this way..." Finally, they will begin to nod their head in agreement with practically everything you say.

Go to www.inventionprep.com to learn how to start profiting off your idea in the next 30 days.

34

If you do this all properly, you'll hear the sweetest question of them all. And that is, "Have you thought about selling the entire business?"

But before you get to this point, you must remember investors are persuaded for different reasons. All want to get a positive return on their money, their way of doing that...and beliefs for how to get there...differ. Therefore, you not only have to choose your target, you must also address their beliefs about HOW to get a return on investment.

For example, my mother is very risk averse so she loves Treasury bonds (even at a lowly 2% return). But my brother in law is in love with the idea of finding the next Google, so has no problem of risking money on new startups.

Now, if you were trying to coax these two people into giving you money, you would approach them much differently, right?

I don't care how slick or skilled of a salesman you are, pitching the wrong prospect won't get you anywhere. Eskimos don't buy ice. The good news is that if you have "the who" correct, you don't even need a great pitch. They'll fill in the blank spots of the part of the pitch you didn't get perfect.

This is why you must research who you are delivering your pitch to, and craft your message accordingly. If you are going on **Shark Tank**, or for

Go to www.inventionprep.com to learn how to
start profiting off your idea in the next 30 days.

35

anyone who pitches any investor, you must know the background of the people you present your product to. There are many ways you can use that to your advantage in the actual pitch (which is what we will go over in the next section). Since the Sharks are TV starts, it's pretty easy to research their public personas, successes and failures, interests, dislikes, upbringing, etc.

With that in mind, I looked up the **Sharks** bios to find out their strengths and weaknesses, and what - if I was sitting in front of them, asking them to invest in my idea - I would need to say to them to make sure my project gets funding.

(Note: you can find their bios on the **Shark Tank** website at www.abc.go.com/shows/shark-tank/bios)

Barbara Corcoran Takeaway:

Barbara proves you don't have to be "book smart" to be successful (D's in high school and college!).

A few years back I ran into an old college buddy of mine. He always finished tests first, straight A's, a wickedly smart guy. Now, jobless. He explained to me about how all of his bosses were too stupid to see his genius.

Can you imagine how well that went over?!

Go to www.inventionprep.com to learn how to start profiting off your idea in the next 30 days.

36

Many of the skills that serve well in highly structured institutions like school (remembering equations, test taking, etc.) will throttle you in the real world. Success isn't about remembering things. It is about forging your own path. Barbara built her empire in the Big Apple, one of the most competitive cities in the world.

If I were attempting to romance an investor like this, I would be frank with my shortcomings...to the point of explaining why they would help in the future. But you can't have a fanciful idea (Barbara pursued real estate, one of the classic - and proven - ways to grow wealth), you must provide solids facts about why you believe your idea is solid.

Finally, I'd exude passion about my products and even hint at a little desire to "prove all my doubters" wrong.

Daymond John Takeaway:

There is one sentence in Daymond John's biography that sticks out. *"One day in 1992, he and his friend sold $800 worth of hats and realized their ideas had definite potential."*
It does not say Daymond had an idea for hats he thought people would love, and then went seeking investors. No, he had an idea, learned how to create it (sewing), and hit the streets to sell it.

Go to www.inventionprep.com to learn how to start profiting off your idea in the next 30 days.

37

$800 is not massive success, but it is proof that people were willing to exchange money for his creations. Sales. Money. Orders. Proof!

Of all the **Shark Tank** episodes I've watched, Daymond always asks about sales...but it does not necessarily have to be huge sales. Just a little bit to prove the concept. He wants to know what you have done to convince consumers to part with their hard earned money.

Is your product in stores? Have you sold a few items at a flea market? Moved product on a website?

If not, I would recommend engineering a strategy (we will go over some later) to get SOME sales before approaching an investor like this.

Kevin O'Leary Takeaway:

Hidden gold mines...vast untapped markets...obscene potential for profits may get the greed glands of some investors going, but you're wasting your time if you show investors like O'Leary anything other than money.

He doesn't want promises, he wants proof. He wants to see where you've made something happen...and how he can swoop in and make a killing off of your hard work (in the process, probably making you very rich too).

Go to www.inventionprep.com to learn how to start profiting off your idea in the next 30 days.

So what do you do when sitting down with a Kevin O'Leary? When pitching your idea, plan on answering questions about money like:

- What are your sales? In what time frame?
- How much do you make your product for?
- How much do you sell your product for? Wholesale? Retail?
- What are you going to do with the money?
- What are your plans for expansion?
- How long do you think it will take me to recoup my investment? To collect a return?

Remember, if you can show Kevin O'Leary the money, he is in. Don't waste time on anything else.

Lori Greiner Takeaway:

Laurie's biography reminds me of the time NASA spent $$$ million on a pen. Here's the story.

NASA discovered ordinary pens would not work in space. Without gravity, the ink would not flow from the pen. So they set their engineers to work. X years and x million dollars later they had a pen that would work in space. Russian astronauts faced the same problem. Do you know how the Russian space program solved the same problem? With a pencil!

Go to www.inventionprep.com to learn how to start profiting off your idea in the next 30 days.

Simple solutions to problems defines Lauries' approach to the world. But unlike the astronaut pen, Laurie loves products with a mass market, everyman appeal that solve small everyday problems...and do so at an affordable price. This means Laurie loves simple, easy to use household products (she has hundreds of them.)

The point here is every investor has angles of making money they are comfortable with. If I was pitching my idea to Laurie, I would explain how it fits into her affordable, everyday problem solving approach (or how it could be bundled with an existing product to boost sales).

Mark Cuban Takeaway:

How do you bust into an established industry and compete with (and beat) the big dogs?

Be different!

Cuban decked out the Mavericks stadium with additional features to transform agame into a big immersive event. He released movies in home the SAME DAY as in theatres. He creates content that normal TV stations won't touch. His competitive strategy is being different.

With the urge to fit in and act "professional", being different is vastly underrated. Sometimes just acting a

Go to www.inventionprep.com to learn how to start profiting off your idea in the next 30 days.

40

little odd is enough to stick out in a marketplace. If you don't believe me study guys like Virgin Records owner Sir Richard Branson or Go Daddy founder Bob Parsons.

Some investors love different for differents sake. Show how your product approaches a problem differently...the unique way it fills a market void...or how it violates industry norms, and you may find success with an investor like Cuban.

Robert Herjavec Takeaway:

I've decided to place Herjavec last on this list because he likes businesses with a "feel good" component to them. But this in and of itself is not enough to sway an investor. A feel good story helps, but you also need what I call the **Aqueduct Factor.**

Here's what I mean.

By the 3rd century, Rome supplied one million citizens with water for public baths, latrines, fountains and even private homes. It was not pumped or shipped in, rather, it flowed in naturally from a variety of distance sources...all due to an elaborate series of aqueducts. Most were buried beneath the ground, and followed its contours; obstructing peaks were circumvented or less often, tunneled through. Where valleys or lowlands intervened, the conduit was carried on bridgework, or its contents fed into high-

Go to www.inventionprep.com to learn how to start profiting off your idea in the next 30 days.

41

pressure lead, ceramic or stone pipes and siphoned across. Most aqueduct systems included sedimentation tanks, sluices and distribution tanks to regulate the supply at need.

Over hills and valleys, through mountains, bridges, and holding tanks. Sounds complex, right? Yes, but this vast system worked due to a simple natural law. Gravity. The aqueducts were built along a slight downward gradient, so the water naturally flowed towards the city. Water ebbs and flows according to the natural law of gravity.

You probably take this fact for granted. It is fairly easy to turn on a faucet...watch water fall and drain...and to conclude this fact for yourself.

But here is a new idea for you to consider. Could the movement of money be governed by simple laws as well? Perhaps money - like water - ebbs and flows due to rules beyond what you currently know? And that maybe if you simply what this law was, and how to apply these rules in your life, you could cause riches to flow to you as easily, and consistently, as the aqueducts delivered water to Rome?

I believe there is such a law. And if you learn the rules of this law and put them to work in your life, the money is sure to flow freely. If you ignore, then money will forever escape your grasp. Let's take a closer look.

Go to www.inventionprep.com to learn how to start profiting off your idea in the next 30 days.

Go to www.inventionprep.com to learn how to
start profiting off your idea in the next 30 days.

43

Part 3: What Creates an Irresistible Idea

Sex, Alcohol, and Lawlessness for Profit, Why Money Moves Toward (or Away) from You and The Aqueduct Factors Continued

When I was in my early twenties I worked for a guy (we'll call him Tim) who pulled in $91,000 a year while working roughly 4 hours a night.

On the surface, you'd think Tim was a bum. Young, usually unshaven and in flip flops, he dropped out of college to start a business centered around the "nightlife" scene. His employees would start work by drinking a few beers...break numerous laws all throughout the night ...and would spend the last hour on the job hitting on drunk girls (actually, we would spend ALL night hitting on drunk girls).

Yet Tim took home more money than most professionals.

My job was that of a bicycle taxi driver (a rickshaw). I would pedal for 3-6 hours a night, shuttling partygoers from one side of the strip to the other. I usually made at least $100 a night. And on the big event nights - like Halloween - I would bring in at

Go to www.inventionprep.com to learn how to start profiting off your idea in the next 30 days.

44

least $2,000. The 5-10 of us who worked each night would fork over a percentage of our earnings (on average $50 a night) while my buddy just organized everything.

I'm using rough numbers here, but at 5 guys a night at $50 a pop, that works out to $1,750 a week. Or roughly $91,000 a year. Let that sink in for a moment. He made $91,000 running a bike taxi business. With uneducated, always drunk, sometimes high, flaky employees who would ditch work in a heartbeat at the first sign of a nice piece of ass.

Not exactly your model workforce. Yet his take home pay placed him firmly in the top 25% of U.S. income earners. Not bad for a few hours at night while working with a bunch of degenerates and partying on the strip all night.

A Few Inconvenient Truths About Money

Here I will present to you some inconvenient truths about money. Some will accept these rules as reality...more will be skeptic...many will find them absolutely repulsive. I do not present these to irritate, annoy, or challenge beliefs, rather in the hope that sharing them with you will help you achieve higher income.

The facts:

Go to www.inventionprep.com to learn how to start profiting off your idea in the next 30 days.

45

- Money does not automatically go to people with fancy degree. There are plenty professionals in well respected positions in this country - doctors, lawyers, engineers - who do much more important and meaningful work than Tim with the bicycle taxi business. Yet, they do not make $91,000. And probably work more. Many, based on how much they work on an hourly basis at least, probably make closer to minimum wage.

- Money does not go where it is needed. Beggars - with raggedly clothes and empty stomachs - surely need the money in my pocket more than I do. Yet, the dollars bills in my wallet do not march out to them. The change in my pocket stays put.

- Money does not go to people who want it. Regularly I come across people who profess to want things...jewelry, fancy clothes and cars, nice vacations. These things do not magically appear. Neither does money.

- Money does not go to people who "should" get it (or even deserve it). Every day children with cancer cannot afford life saving treatments, and die. This is unfortunate. They do not deserve to have their lives cut short. Yet, money does march forth to help their plight.

Go to www.inventionprep.com to learn how to start profiting off your idea in the next 30 days.

46

I understand these might not be nice concepts to think about. Maybe you are thinking it "shouldn't" be this way. Or it's not fair.

If so, I agree with you. I thought that way for years. When I graduated college with a "fancy" mechanical engineering degree I thought the world would be banging a path to my door because of the time and money I invested in my degree and the skills I learned. Boy was I in for a rude awakening when I hit the "real world". My first engineering job paid $15 an hour.

So where does money go?

The shortest explanation I've heard is: Money goes to people who offer things to the world that other people find more valuable than the money in their pocket. That's it. This is a point so immensely important that it should not be glossed over. I repeat. Money goes to people who offer things to the world that other people find more valuable than the money in their pocket.

I heard these concepts first from Dan Kennedy (as a side not, he is worthy of study). I'm not sure what he calls it, but I call them the **Money Motion Laws.** And yes, these are irrefutable laws of nature. If you were to observe, you would find these laws to be as consistent as the law of gravity itself.

Go to www.inventionprep.com to learn how to start profiting off your idea in the next 30 days.

47

The one big exception to this law is when outright theft occurs.

But that is not money moving naturally TO them. That is force, effort. It takes work fighting AGAINST a natural law. Let's put this in the context of the natural law of gravity. How much easier is it to pedal a bike downhill - with gravity - than pedal a bike uphill against gravity?

Of course it is easier to coast downhill. This effort is the difference between working against - instead of with - the natural **Money Motion Law**.

Again, the law states: Money goes to people who offer things to the world that other people find more valuable than the money in their pocket. A few examples:

- Money moves to the person selling bottled water to the thirsty
- Money moves to the electric company that ensures a constant flow of energy into your house
- Money moves from the parents to the university in the hopes their child will become more prepared for the real world
- Money moves to the movie star that transports you away from your real life for awhile into an exciting fantasy

Go to www.inventionprep.com to learn how to start profiting off your idea in the next 30 days.

48

- Money moves to the salesman who provides a car to those in need of transport (or if it is a fancy car like a Ferrari, to those in need of showing off and stroking their ego)
- Money moves to the prostitute that provides a few hours of fun
- Money moves to the corrupt cop who is paid off by the drug dealers so they can push drugs without police interference

You'll notice some of these examples are illegal (in some places). But you'll find it hard to argue that they do not happen. They are natural laws. Not man-made laws. "Good" or "Bad", they are important illustrations then. The movement of money has nothing to do with education, ethics, time invested, needs, wants, seniority, corruption, man-made laws, or morals. It moves when people who offer things to the world that other people find more valuable than the money in their pocket.

Why People Buy

If you take a closer look at these examples, you'll notice a formula emerges.

First, find a desire - Everyone desires something. Young boys desire action figures, teenage girls desire tickets to boy band concerts, middle aged men desire sports cars, adult women desire Louis Vuitton purses.

Go to www.inventionprep.com to learn how to start profiting off your idea in the next 30 days.

49

These are niche examples. Products with mass market appeal fulfill a mass market desire.

One of the best recent examples is the rise of the Apple IPad and the mass market desire for instant consumption of entertainment. Before the IPad, you entertained yourself via TV, books, on your cell phone or through your computer. But TV was static (usually you had it just in your home), books required going to the store or library before you could read them, the cell phone screen is small (making it difficult to fully enjoy entertainment), and computers takes too long to boot up to access the internet.

Second, create something to fulfill that desire - Other than life's necessities like basic nutrition, water, and shelter, most objects are an avenue to fulfill a desire.

Action figures transport young boys into the fantasy land of action and adventure. Teenage girls love boy bands because they speak to the emotions of raging hormones (you'd be surprised by the lyrics of a Justin Beiber song) . Middle aged men desire sports cars because it reminds them of their youth. I have no clue why adult women love Louis Vuitton purses, but I guess it has something to do with showing off to their friends.

The iPad fulfilled the desire for instant, affordable, and portable entertainment. Now you don't have to

Go to www.inventionprep.com to learn how to start profiting off your idea in the next 30 days.

50

wait 2 minutes for your computer to boot up so you can access the internet. You don't have to be at home to watch TV, go to a movie theatre to see a movie, or head to the local library to get a book.

The lesson is: The IPad was not a success because it was a new fancy gadget. It took the world by storm because it fulfilled the almost universal desire of instant gratification.

Third, find the optimum selling strategy - This involves the who, what, why, where, when, and how.

- Who are you selling to?
- What are they actually buying (your product, your service, your expertise)?
- Why are they buying (that is the desire I talked about above)?
- Where are they buying (retail stores, flea markets, 1-800 numbers on TV commercials, showrooms, thru ads in magazines, by mail)?
- When (time of day, week, month, year, seasonal) do they buy?
- How do they buy (via cash, credit, layaway, barter)?

This is not as easy as it sounds. Take clothes for example. You could argue the reason people buy clothes is so they don't run around naked. But if that was the truth, why aren't we all running around in the

Go to www.inventionprep.com to learn how to start profiting off your idea in the next 30 days.

51

cheapest clothes available? If clothes were just to cover up, there would be no reason for $90 t-shirts, $300 designer jeans, and $1,000 shoes.

It's true some people buy clothes just to cover up. And others buy clothes to express their personal style. Some buy to show off. Some buy for work purposes. Some for play.

Now ask yourself a question. How and where are these different types of clothes sold? How is selling a three piece suit different from selling a camouflage jacket used by hunters? How are leather motorcycle jackets sold compared to bikinis? Would a woman buy a t-shirt off a website before buying it? How about a wedding dress?

The answers to these questions reveal the strategy behind selling the products that these certain groups of people desire.

To recap, the **Money Motion Law** states money moves when people who offer things to the world that other people find more valuable than the money in their pocket (except in the case of theft, which is using force to oppose this natural law). And the three steps to getting this law to work for you are:

1. Find a Desire
2. Create Something to Fulfill that Desire
3. Find the Optimum Way to Sell it.

Go to www.inventionprep.com to learn how to start profiting off your idea in the next 30 days.

52

Now let's dig a little deeper, get to the real nitty gritty stuff, and explore how contestant on the show persuaded investors to back their product.

The Aqueduct Factors

After watching nearly all of the episodes on *Shark Tank* I noticed a pattern emerge among the winners. No matter how different their idea, product, or invention was, each product pitch contained four similar elements...the **Aqueduct Factors** (named after the aqueducts in Rome that naturally guided water to the city).

When a pitch did not include one or two of these elements, the *Sharks* flushed them like waste from a bilge tank. When a pitch included all four elements the *Sharks* practically tripped over themselves fighting to invest in the product.

It was like the Marvel Comic Book group *The Fantastic Four.* The bad guys could probably overpower just one of them. But when all four teamed up they were unbeatable.

If you use these four **Aqueduct Factors,** you'll spend less time pitching your idea/invention/product and more time trying to figure out what to do with all the money you get.

Let's dig in...

Go to www.inventionprep.com to learn how to start profiting off your idea in the next 30 days.

53

The Aqueduct Factor Element #1:
"A Horse, A Horse, My Kingdom For A Horse!"

This famous line comes from act 5, scene 4 of Shakespeare's play Richard III. The hunchbacked villain-king Richard III is about to meet his doom at the hands of the future Henry VII and begs for escape.

Tweezers pull thorns out. Band-Aids help cuts heal. Home pregnancy tests...
The world is full of problems. And if you have a solution to that problem there is money to be made.

When I was a kid my job was to mow the lawn. And in South Florida, grass grows faster than a speeding bullet. I literally had to mow the lawn twice a week, almost every week of my life until I moved out at 18.

Once I moved out, I swore I would never mow another lawn again. But I have a problem...the grass still grows. So how do I solve that problem? I hire people to do it.

People will gladly pay to solve their problems.

The **Sharks** know this. And that is why they love products that solve problems. Kevin O'leary summed it up best when he pointed out that a successful product comes from two things: 1. Solving

Go to www.inventionprep.com to learn how to start profiting off your idea in the next 30 days.

problems. 2. Reducing costs. Notice the first one is solving problems.

So the first Aqueduct Factor is Solve a Problem!

But there is a catch here (and it is one most novice inventors completely ignore...to their financial peril). Your product or idea must solve a problem worth paying to solve. Nobody is going to shell out big money for trivial matters. Expensive inventions must solve BIG problems. Or small problem solvers must be cheap!

For example. I hate having to move my clothes from the washer to the dryer. But it's a hell of a lot better than cleaning by hand (and worth the few hundred dollar investment in machines). And yes, I hate having to remove lint from my clothes dryer filter. But would I pay for something that would suck it out for me? Only if it cost pennies per use.

And sure, I could just pay someone to do my laundry...but it doesn't bother me so much it is worth the extra money (unless of course I just have to have a certain shirt to wear that night).

So...how do you know if your solution is worth paying for? Or paying a lot for?

Two words pain and urgency.

Go to www.inventionprep.com to learn how to start profiting off your idea in the next 30 days.

55

A problem grows bigger as the pain and urgency increase. And as the problem grows, so does the willingness to pay to make it go away. This is why doctors can charge so much. If there is physical pain mixed with life threatening urgency...people will pay almost anything.

With this in mind let's see how entrepreneurs on **Shark Tank** used the problem/solution formula to pitch their products:

- Smartbaker
  - Problem: How to scale recipies
  - Solution: Apron with built in cheat sheet and measurements
- Profender
  - Problem: Difficult to realistically practice basketball against moving defenders without other people to practice with
  - Solution: Movable, height adjustable "dummy" defenders
- Citi Kitty
  - Problem: messy cat litter inside the house
  - Solution: Toilet train your cat
- Onesoles
  - Problem: Too many shoes
  - Solution: One sole for a shoe, with multiple, interchangeable tops
- Last Lid

Go to www.inventionprep.com to learn how to start profiting off your idea in the next 30 days.

- Problem: Lost/Stolen lid off trash can
- Solution: Universal fit fabric trash can lid
- Carsik Bib
  - Problem: Sick kids in car
  - Solution: Bib with built in throw up bag
- Sweep Easy
  - Problem: Brooms can't remove stuff stuck to floor
  - Solution: Broom with built in scraper
- Ride on Carry On
  - Problem: Difficult to travel with small children
  - Solution: Seat for children built into rolling luggage

Aqueduct Factor Element #2:
How 13 Words Led to $25 Billion

The Russian craft "Sputnick" was the first satellite ever launched into space. Embarrassed by the early space success of their cold war enemies, U.S. President John F. Kennedy vowed to beat the Soviet Union and put the first man on the moon.

With hundreds of satellites, private space flight, and robots on Mars, this may seem commonplace - even quaint - by today's standards.

Go to www.inventionprep.com to learn how to start profiting off your idea in the next 30 days.

But think about it back then. Never before in the history of our species had mankind made it off this rock. To put a man on the moon was big, bold, daring, different. An adventure of epic proportions. On May 25, 1961 Kennedy spoke 13 simple words, stating a big, audacious goal for the U.S., "landing a man on the Moon and returning him safely to the Earth". On July 20, 1969, that goal became a reality.

The numbers say it took $25 billion dollars, close to a decade, and the collective effort of an army of engineers, technicians, and hard labor to put two men on the moon.

But the spark that lit that decade of work and investment was ignited by a big idea.

The second Aqueduct Factor is Have a Big Idea. You do not have to put a man on the moon, but your invention or product needs to be driven by an idea (preferably a big one, definitely not a small one).

I learned of this concept from a mentor of mine, Mark Ford (who also goes by the pen name Michael Masterson). He works with a company called Agora Publishing. Agora primarily publishes newsletters, which are sold by long salesletters....sometimes letters as long as 50 pages in length. Each year they write thousands of these letters to promote their services.

Go to www.inventionprep.com to learn how to start profiting off your idea in the next 30 days.

If that sounds like a "boring" company, you should know they net about $500 million in sales every year.

Anyway, Mark said he stumped upon the power of the Big Idea after researching the most successful letters written in the company. The gangbuster promotions that pulled in one, five, even twenty million dollars in sales. He said about 90% of these letters contained and focused on just one big idea.

This doesn't surprise me. Breakthrough products, the ones changing the way people live, work, and play...in fact ripping apart old ways of thinking and doing, and in the process supercharging cultural evolution (and revolutions) are driven by big ideas.

- Cell phones- what could be bigger than allowing anyone, anywhere the ability to instantly communicate with anyone on the planet?
- Radio and TV- Did you know the most watched TV broadcast featured Elvis Presley? Communication on a mass scale. Before, you had to amass people in one place to get your message out. With radio and TV, one person can impact millions around the world. Radio did this via sound only. TV included the visual aspect.
- Electricity - power to the people, the ability to run hundreds of thousands of gadgets that make life easier. If it wasn't for electricity

Go to www.inventionprep.com to learn how to start profiting off your idea in the next 30 days.

59

many of the modern conveniences - dishwashers, laundry cleaners, garbage disposals, those little lights in the refrigerator, power tools, home computers, flashlights, garage door openers, ad infinitum - would not be possible.

Boats, metallurgy, gunpowder, the cotton gin, cars, planes, the atomic bomb, the internet, even Facebook and Twitter.

These inventions changed the lives of billions of people because of the big ideas driving them. Investors LOVE big ideas. Who invested in cell technology? Radio and TV? And one of the richest men in the world, JP Morgan bet the farm on electricity.

Come to the **Shark Tank** with a Big Idea, and the **Sharks** will surely listen. Now, take a look at a few "big idea" driven products presented on **Shark Tank**.

- Kisstix
  - Big Idea: Chap stick that creates a new flavor when two people kiss
- Ledge Pillow
  - Big Idea: Speciality pillow to help women with large breast implants sleep easier
- Aldo Orta Designs

Go to www.inventionprep.com to learn how to start profiting off your idea in the next 30 days.

60

- o Big Idea: Very fancy jewelry combining many religious iconography images
- Talbott Teas
  - o Big Idea: Designer whole leaf teas (note: this was not being done at the time. Like when Ben and Jerry's reinvented how ice cream was sold)
- M3 Girl Designs
  - o Big Idea: Jewelry made of bottlecaps with magnets on back, so you can move bottlecaps from one piece to another
- Games 2U
  - o Big Idea: Franchised Mobile Entertainment Company - bring fun games to parties, corporate events, etc.
- DaisyCakes
  - o Big Idea: Tasty desserts delivered to your door

Aqueduct Factor Element #3:
The $1.7 Billion Dollar Piranha

The big bad wolf and three little pigs. Darth Vader and Luke Skywalker. Prince charming.

If you've ever heard of these characters, you already know the story. I don't need to recount the huffing and the puffing and the blowing down of the house. Or about the tale of redemption and family of

Go to www.inventionprep.com to learn how to start profiting off your idea in the next 30 days.

61

Star Wars. Or of Prince Charming fulfilling every girls fantasy of being swept away by the man of her dreams.

Stories burn memories into your brain. And stories sell. Weave a compelling yarn and people will buy your product and investors will fund your projects.

Sure, you could just say your new laundry detergent cleans clothes. Or you could tell the tale of how...just hours before a first date with her future husband...Margaret spilled wine on her brand new $300 dress...and the only thing that could clean the garment (and ensure Margaret lands her future husband) was your detergent.

Which do you think is more compelling?

The third Aqueduct Factor is storytelling.

In fact, one of the greatest ad campaigns used stories to pitch a cheap, disposable product. Allow me to set the scene...

A suited man is talking to another man about his beloved fish tank. In the suited man's hands are two plastic sandwich bags. Each bag is filled with water and...piranhas! Now here is the punch line. One bag has a regular clear zipping seal, the other has the famous zip-lock yellow and blue make green seal so that you KNOW it is sealed.

Go to www.inventionprep.com to learn how to start profiting off your idea in the next 30 days.

62

The question...if you were to drop ONE of those bags in the first tank, which would you TRUST to be absolutely, positively sealed? The clear seal or the yellow and blue make green seal? Which bag would you rely upon if you didn't want those piranhas to escape and devour your precious little fishies?

To give you an idea of how much zip lock is worth, in 1997 Dow Chemical sold the rights of DowBrands, which included Ziploc, to SC Johnson for between $1.3 and $1.7 billion dollars.

Stories grab attention, intrigue, and best of all...stories keep people engaged. (Which is one of the reasons I love stories! Go back through this report and you'll notice I've sprinkled stories throughout the text to - hopefully - keep you reading. If you are reading this now it is proof that stories work.)

So, how do you tell a story?

There are as many formulas as there are stories, but the most basic is the three-act structure. It is a model which divides stories into three parts called the Setup, the Confrontation and the Resolution.

Basically, the setup explains the heroes of the story and their environment. The confrontation explains what their problems are. And the resolutions explain how they overcame those problems.

This classic formula can be found everywhere.

Go to www.inventionprep.com to learn how to start profiting off your idea in the next 30 days.

Frodo Baggins must destroy the evil ring in *The Lord of the Rings* Trilogy. The Autobots battle the Decepticons in *Transformers*. Gigi Haim (played by Ginnifer Goodwin) confronts her own inner insecurities in *He's Just Not That Into You*.

Here's how a few products on **Shark Tank** have been presented with the classic three part story structure:

- Hydromax
  - The story: Kids playing football who dehydrate on the field due to lack of adequate hydration. And how his invention, a water filled bladder that fits in football shoulder pads, would fix this problem.
- Nardo's Naturals
  - The story: A mom (who is a skin care specialist), told her four sons how to treat a sunburn, and that's how the product was born.
- Due in shirts:
  - The story: A pregnant woman was tired to people asking her when her baby was due. So she made a line of shirts that said "Due in January", "Due in February", etc. so they wouldn't ask her anymore
- Hot Mama Gowns

Go to www.inventionprep.com to learn how to start profiting off your idea in the next 30 days.

64

- The story: A woman noticed how many pregnant women were embarrassed and humiliated when wearing ugly hospital gowns, so she invented a line of stylish and hip gowns for them to wear while having their child.
- Fridge Friends
  - The story: Depressed at an ugly fridge, but not willing to buy another one, they invented a magnetic cover that gave the fridge a "facelift".
- Express Effects Cosmetics
  - The story: A woman was frustrated at how hard it is to lose weight, so she invented a lip gloss that curbs appetite.
- Hill Billy
  - The story: About how people identify with the Hill Billy lifestyle (hunting, off-roading, NASCAR) etc. So they invented a brand of clothing called "Hill Billy"

Aqueduct Factor Element #4:
The Inner Tug of War that Sabotages Inventors

We have a very big problem in society that makes breakthroughs (and to some extent success) damn near impossible.

Go to www.inventionprep.com to learn how to start profiting off your idea in the next 30 days.

65

It starts at home when your parents start teaching you the ABC's. It continues in schools with dress codes and learning curriculums. And continues with the social influence to "fit in with the crowd".

But how can you expect to invent the next new breakthrough product if you are not different, if you don't go against the grain?

Most everybody wants things their way, but - because of this constant push (from the second we pop out of the womb) - most don't get it. In fact, most are persuaded to feel guilt and shame about it. Their desires unreasonable or unfair to others. With constant worry about being criticized or disliked for it.

If you haven't guessed, the problem I am speaking of is the push to conform. Even (ESPECIALLY) when it goes against your true inner desires.

Now, for the record, I don't think all conformity is bad. Imagine if one of your neighbors spoke Spanish, another Japanese, and still another German, how could you guys talk to each other? Probably not. Communication would be impossible if we all had to make up our own languages.

But like all things, strengths can become weaknesses. And most people have been taught (or in some cases manipulated into believing) being different is bad. This line of thinking is poisonous to the human species. Change, evolution, growth

Go to www.inventionprep.com to learn how to start profiting off your idea in the next 30 days.

DEPENDS on thinking, behaving, and acting differently.

Case in point, death and disease in the ancient world...

Before the 19th century, most people believed poisonous vapor or mist filled with particles from decomposed matter caused illness. This was called the Miasma Theory.

The miasmatic position was that diseases were the product of environmental factors such as contaminated water, foul air, and poor hygienic conditions. That it would waft through the air and kill anything in its path.

Then Louis Pasteur proclaimed it wasn't toxic gas causing death and disease, but microscopic bacteria and fungus. Germs. Imagine how well this went over! I can see uneducated crowds with their eyebrows raised saying, "So you're telling me germs are invading my body. But they are so small I can't even see them. No, that's ok. I'll keep believing other dead things are causing my sickness."

And who can blame them? Doesn't it make sense some death things will spread sickness and death? Who would believe something you can't see could be so bad for you? Most people thought he was crazy.

Go to www.inventionprep.com to learn how to start profiting off your idea in the next 30 days.

67

Yet his experiments showed how germs did in fact cause sickness. Today, Pasteur's theory is scientific fact. His doubters have been forgotten by history.

The final Aqueduct Factor is Be Different!

A more current example can be found in pop sensation Justin Beiber. While most musicians would practically kill to be "discovered" and signed by a record company, Beiber went a different route. He was the first to use a new media - YouTube - to grow his fan base. Once he became such a huge sensation on his own, record companies had to take notice.

For more proof, think of all the unique, colorful, peculiar, and sometimes downright odd people raking in oodles of dough. Here are a few off the top of my head:

- Rush Limbaugh
- Tom Cruise
- Howard Stern
- Lindsay Lohan
- Russell Brand
- The Singer Formerly Known as Prince
- Tim Tebow
- Sarah Palin
- Michael Moore
- Lady Gaga
- Michael Jackson

Go to www.inventionprep.com to learn how to start profiting off your idea in the next 30 days.

Odd people all of them. You can call them weird, crazy, chemically imbalanced, or even sociopathic. Whatever, you cannot deny they grab attention. Different catches attention and can lead to fame and fortune. Take a look at how "being different" is presented as a plus in **Shark Tank** episodes:

- Litter Jewelry
  - How it's different: Instead of ordinary jewelry (like necklaces, bracelets, earrings, etc), they create body jewelry for the arms, legs, and even fake moustache jewelry.
- Rent-a-Grandma
  - How it's different: A service that provides grandma aged babysitters.
- Wine Balloon
  - How it's different: Traditional wine stoppers just recork the bottle. The Wine Balloon slips inside the bottle, filling up the space where air usually resides. This prevents wine spoilage, by removing the air that oxidizes wine.
- Chord Buddy
  - How it's different: The device covers up strings on the neck of a guitar, making it absolutely foolproof to play a guitar...perfectly...every time.
- Lightfilm LLC

Go to www.inventionprep.com to learn how to start profiting off your idea in the next 30 days.

69

o   How it's different: It's a decal you put on the back of a car that lights up (via an internal battery).
- Broccoli Wad
  o   How it's different: Instead of a big, bulky wallet, it's just a simple band that holds money together.
- Tec
  o   How it's different: Clothing with multiple pockets for cell phone, laptop, tablet, etc. with built in channels for cords and earbuds (so that cables don't tangle up).

The perfect pitches contain all four of these. A big idea that solves a problem presented in story format that is also different.

A perfect example of this is Chord Buddy. Invented by Travis Perry and a hit on the show, here's how it fits the four criteria...

1. **Problem/solution:** I'm not a guitar player, but I've tried. And I can tell you from experience that it is difficult and confusing to learn all of the different string/chord combination. By blocking out a few strings at a time, the device makes it impossible NOT to play the right chord. Making it easier to learn to play the guitar. (In fact, in the episode where this aired, Mark Herjavec successfully played a

Go to www.inventionprep.com to learn how to start profiting off your idea in the next 30 days.

70

few notes, despite having no clue how to play the guitar.)

2. **Big Idea:** You know you have a big idea when you say "What if..." and someone responds in amazement. In the case of the Chord Buddy, it is "What if you could pick up a guitar for the first time, and play like a pro?" The big idea here is a simple piece of plastic that can help anyone play guitar. Imagine how difficult it is to learn...you've got strings at different lengths on the neck, and different sizes, you have to put your fingers on some, and not others. Waaay confusing. But this makes it simple, which makes it a big idea.

3. **Story:** Travis Perry, the inventor, started out explaining how he was a country singer from LA - Lower Alabama. This got a bunch of laughs, but what really hooked the **Sharks** was when explained how hard it was to learn how to play guitar. And how he wanted to help his children and grandchildren play without all the hassles that he went through. This touched heartstrings of course, but it also demonstrated how passionate he was about solving this particular problem.

4. **Different:** And finally, like I mentioned above, the device covers up strings on the neck of a guitar, making it absolutely foolproof to play a guitar...perfectly...every time.

Go to www.inventionprep.com to learn how to start profiting off your idea in the next 30 days.

71

And what did Travis Perry get for his troubles? Everyone except for Mark Cuban offered to pitch in, and he ended up with a deal with Robert Herjavec for $175,000 for a 20% stake, plus $50,000 set aside for an infomercial.

Do a Google search for Chord Buddy and you'll see just how well they are doing now.
Warning, these formulas do NOT always produce a winner. But those who don't win, rarely contain any of these.

A good example of this is Ecomowers. Inventor Andy Humphrey tried to pitch a push powered lawn mower to the **Sharks**. But these were first invented back in 1827 by a British guy named Edwin Budding. It didn't solve a new problem. There was nothing big behind the idea. There was no story to it and it wasn't different. Looking closer at other **Shark Tank** losers, we'll notice the same trend.

- Uncle Zips Beef Jerky - nothing different from regular beef jerky
- Swilt - basically a hooded jacket (plus a really bad name, in my opinion)
- Liquid Money - a cologne that smells like money
- Heat Helper - recycles heat from your dryer into your house
- CaddySwag - a beer cooler that fits in a golf bag

Go to www.inventionprep.com to learn how to start profiting off your idea in the next 30 days.

- Tail Lights - ornamental lights that stick on back pockets of jeans
- New Era Brands - gum mints in a case

Yes, some of these contain elements of the four formulas listed above.

The Heat Helper would save money by recycling heat from the dryer into the house (and yes, not being able to save money is a problem for many people). But would the little bit of heat from the dryer be able to save THAT much money? I don't think so.

If you want a winning pitch (or to produce a winning product) solve a BIG problem - not a little one. Have a BIG IDEA not a little one. Tell a compelling story. And be different.

Remember the **Aqueduct Factors** and you'll be well on your way to delivering a winning pitch.

Go to www.inventionprep.com to learn how to start profiting off your idea in the next 30 days.

73

Final Thoughts

How to Make This System
Work for You

At the beginning of this report I introduced you to a quote from Thomas Edison about success. He said, *"Anything that won't sell, I don't want to invent. Its sale is proof of utility, and utility is success"*.

I love this quote because it really sums up the difference between failure and success, the crazy tinkerer who toils and never finishes anything vs. the respected innovator who sees his products on store shelves across the country. There are plenty of things you COULD invent...perhaps a device that will automatically wash your cat...or would tell you when your underwear is dirty...or dump a cold bucket of water on you every morning to help you get out of bed.

But that doesn't mean people will buy it.

Success, then, doesn't automatically stem from simply inventing. It comes from creating products that people cannot live without. That people want to buy. That people fall over themselves to invest in. And if you simply follow the steps revealed in this report (the steps most inventors overlook) you'll be well on your way to doing just that.

Go to www.inventionprep.com to learn how to start profiting off your idea in the next 30 days.

If you've read this beginning to end you now know how to:

- Successfully answer the 9 questions investors want to know about sales
- Address investors concerns about your product, plan, or you (the Three P's of Inventor Financing)
- Plant the seed of success by creating vision and using Entrepreneurial Alchemy
- Save tons of time, money, and energy by pitching to the right person
- Create products that people want to buy because of the Money Motion Law
- And know how to pitch those products by demonstrating how they solve a problem, contain a big ideas, using stories, and how they are different (the four Aqueduct Factors)

One of the challenges I faced in writing this report was finding examples from **Shark Tank** that fit ALL the rules I laid out here in a step by step format. Why was it difficult? Because most of the "winners" did not get everything perfect. Some of them didn't solve big problems. Some of them weren't driven by a big idea. Some of them had no plans for moving forward. Many of them could not answer one single question about sales.

If they couldn't do it...and could still sway the Sharks to invest with them - then this is good news for

Go to www.inventionprep.com to learn how to start profiting off your idea in the next 30 days.

75

you! What it means is you do not need to have all your ducks in a row either. You do not have to be perfect. It means you just have to do what you've read here, get a few things right (not everything), and you'll find yourself leagues ahead of other inventors.

If you do this I promise you things will go your way. You'll spend less time working on the products no one will ever buy. You won't invest your own money in "duds". Investors will love your ideas. Customers will love your products.

Now I understand this isn't always the easiest thing in the world to do.

Many inventors are so "close" to their invention that it is difficult for them to step back and see the big picture.

So...then...the difficult (and time consuming part) for them become not actually inventing things. But digging out the most persuasive elements... and...presenting them in a way that is appealing to investors (who are actively looking for good ideas to invest in).

That's where I come in. I help people who have ideas and inventions (just like you) create presentation to persuade investors to back your ideas.

And if you're not ready to present to investors just yet, I can show you:

Go to www.inventionprep.com to learn how to start profiting off your idea in the next 30 days.

- How to save thousands of dollars on legal fees while patenting your invention
- How to find designers and engineers to create your ideas on paper and in real life (from sketches to prototypes, to mass manufacturing) quicker than you ever dreamed possible
- And, how to get all the money you need WITHOUT investors...usually within 30 days (AND you get to keep ALL your equity)

Most people think it takes a major investment of time and money to get their ideas off the ground.

Now you can start profiting from your ideas and inventions in as little as 30 days.

If you'd like me to help, just send an email to Rob@inventionprep.com and we'll take it from there.

Go to www.inventionprep.com to learn how to start profiting off your idea in the next 30 days.

77

Appendix A: Checklist

1)   **If you have sales you must be able to answer these 9 questions:**
   a) How much in sales do you have?
   b) How long did it take to make those sales?
   c) What were the sales first year, next year, year after that, etc.?
   d) What's the margin?
   e) How much do you have in unfilled orders?
   f) Where are you selling this?
   g) What's your profit margin (cost to make vs. cost to sell – sell to retail or end user)?
   h) What's your projection for sales (1 year from now...2 years from now, etc.)?
   i) And the best question – Would you sell the whole business?

2)   **Perform Entrepreneurial Alchemy by creating vision of what you are doing**
   a) The Three P's of Inventor Financing (WHAT vision are you creating?)
      i)   *Product*
         (1) Who is it for?
         (2) When does your target need this product?
         (3) Liability?
         (4) How are you different? How is this unique? What's proprietary?

Go to www.inventionprep.com to learn how to start profiting off your idea in the next 30 days.

78

(5) How much do you have in unfilled orders?

(6) Do you make this yourself or with help?

(7) What proprietary technology (patents/trademarks/copyrights) do you have?

(8) What's the margin?

(9) Walk me through how it works?

ii)   *Plan*

(1) What are you going to do in 5 years?

(2) When does your target need this product?

(3) How will you get there?

(4) Walk me through how it works?

(5) What would you do with the money?

(6) Where do you want to sell this?

(7) Do you make this yourself or with help?

iii)   *Personal*

(1) What is your motivation?

(2) How did you get into this business?

(3) How much of your own time/money have you put into it?

(4) Have you gone to a bank to try and get money?

(5) Have you paid yourself?

3)   **Who are you pitching?**

Go to www.inventionprep.com to learn how to start profiting off your idea in the next 30 days.

79

a) Most inventors fail to secure funding NOT because they don't have great ideas, but because they fail to communicate the value of those ideas to the right people in the right way.

4)   Money - like water - ebbs and flows due to rules

a) Money does not automatically go to people with fancy degree. There are plenty professionals in well respected positions in this country - doctors, lawyers, engineers - who do much more important and meaningful work than Tim with the bicycle taxi business. Yet, they do not make $91,000. And probably work more. Many, based on how much they work on an hourly basis at least, probably make closer to minimum wage.

b) Money does not go where it is needed. Beggars - with raggedly clothes and empty stomachs - surely need the money in my pocket more than I do. Yet, the dollars bills in my wallet do not march out to them. The change in my pocket stays put.

c) Money does not go to people who want it. Regularly I come across people who profess to want things...jewelry, fancy clothes and cars, nice vacations. These things do not magically appear. Neither does money.

d) Money does not go to people who "should" get it (or even deserve it). Every day children with cancer cannot afford life saving treatments, and die. This is unfortunate. They

Go to www.inventionprep.com to learn how to start profiting off your idea in the next 30 days.

80

do not deserve to have their lives cut short. Yet, money does march forth to help their plight.

5)   **The Money Motion Law**
   a) Find a Desire
   b) Create Something to Fulfill that Desire
   c) Find the Optimum Way to Sell it.

6)   **The Aqueduct Factors: How to get the Money Motion law to work for you**

   a) Problem/Solution: Your product or idea must solve a problem worth paying to solve. Nobody is going to shell out big money for trivial matters. Expensive inventions must solve BIG problems. Or small problem solvers must be cheap!

   b) Big Idea: Your invention or product needs to be driven by an idea (preferably a big one, definitely not a small one). Investors LOVE big ideas. Who invested in cell technology? Radio and TV? And one of the richest men in the world, JP Morgan bet the farm on electricity.

   c) Story: Stories grab attention, intrigue, and best of all...stories keep people engaged until they buy.

   d) Different: Change, evolution, growth DEPENDS on thinking, behaving, and acting differently. Different catches attention and can lead to fame and fortune.

Go to www.inventionprep.com to learn how to start profiting off your idea in the next 30 days.

81

Appendix B: *Shark Tank* Quotes

"Your projection of $4.8 million dollars with no justification of how to get there really makes us have to be foolish to believe you." – Barbara Corcoran (on Nardo's Naturals, which she invested in)

"Time is the most precious asset" – Mark Cuban

"With the size of the market at $199 retail, I just don't see it. I'm out" – Kevin O'Leary (on the Profender basketball training system)

"I'm going to give you nothing. You have no sales. You don't even have good packaging. There's nothing proprietary or unique about this product. You're going to get slaughtered. I'm out." – Kevin O'Leary

"How can we ramp this up?" – Kevin O'Leary

"Money always controls everything. All of the time." – Kevin O'Leary

"85% of U.S. businesses just provide an income for the owner. But that's not an investible business." – Robert Herjavec

"The lion's share (of profits) is going direct to the consumer, because that's where you're going to make the highest margin." – Lori Greiner

Go to www.inventionprep.com to learn how to start profiting off your idea in the next 30 days.

"The only thing that really matters – what is it – money." – Kevin O'Leary

"If you believe in the product, why don't you put your own money into it?" – Robert Herjavec

"This is where I made all of my money…licensing out my brands." – Daymond John

"We all have a dream. And just like every dream has a price…every dream has a shelf life." – Robert Herjavec

"Never answer a sales question with what you sold over 3 years. Makes me think your sales aren't good. What have you sold in the last 12 months?" – Robert Herjavec

"I think you're smart enough to understand the power of the (trade)mark. That there is a great business in and of itself." – Daymond John

"You can only have one vision. You can't have 15." – Kevin O'Leary

"It's tough to write a check for someone who isn't eating, sleeping and breathing the business." – Mark Cuban

"25 years ago, getting up at 5 o'clock in the morning, doing 15 radio shows, doing redneck jokes

Go to www.inventionprep.com to learn how to start profiting off your idea in the next 30 days.

83

trying to develop that brand." – Jeff Foxworthy (on brands)

Go to www.inventionprep.com to learn how to start profiting off your idea in the next 30 days.

84

Awesome Free Bonuses!

Visit www.inventionprep.com for free instant access to more free cool stuff like...

- Personal feedback from licensed patent professionals, engineers, and experienced marketers on how to protect, create, and sell your idea.
- How to save thousands on legal fees to protect your idea
- Quickly and cheaply create prototypes and final products (in days instead of weeks or months)
- Profit from your idea as quick as humanely possible...usually inside 30 days

Just go to www.inventionprep.com for instant access.

Go to www.inventionprep.com to learn how to start profiting off your idea in the next 30 days.

85

www.ingramcontent.com/pod-product-compliance
Lightning Source LLC
Chambersburg PA
CBHW071754170526
45167CB00003B/1031